Classical Vases and Containers
in the Collection of the Seattle Art Museum

Lawrence J. Bliquez

This publication has been generously supported by grants from the National Endowment for the Arts and PONCHO.

Printed in Japan
ISBN 0-932216-19-6
LC 85-50711
Designed by Corinna Campbell

cover: Kylix by Xenokles (from Etruria), 550-530 B.C.; exterior: bull and deer, interior: rooster and hen. H: 4 ⅜" *SAM 59.100*

Foreword

Norman Davis has spent nearly forty years in pursuit of eloquent objects from the ancient Mediterranean world; the Norman and Amelia Davis Classical Collection of the Seattle Art Museum is the fortuitous result.

Mr. Davis's love for Greek art was first kindled in 1928 by lunch-hour walks to the British Museum from his nearby business office. Moving to Seattle in 1938, Mr. Davis maintained contact with British antiquities curators and dealers during return visits to a London apartment each summer. An initial purchase of a ceramic Greek figure in London after World War II was followed by avid acquisition in other areas of classical art, particularly Greek numismatics. By 1955 the growing collection prompted Mrs. Davis to remark that "the piano was getting overloaded," and Mr. Davis, then vice-president of the museum's board of trustees, approached Dr. Richard E. Fuller with an initial gift of treasured coins and ceramics. Gifts of successive years grew to the over 180 objects now in the collection, which is housed in a gallery furnished with permanent cases generously donated by Mr. Davis in 1966. The Seattle Art Museum is pleased to document a part of this significant collection with this publication.

Gail Joice
Registrar, Head of Museum Services

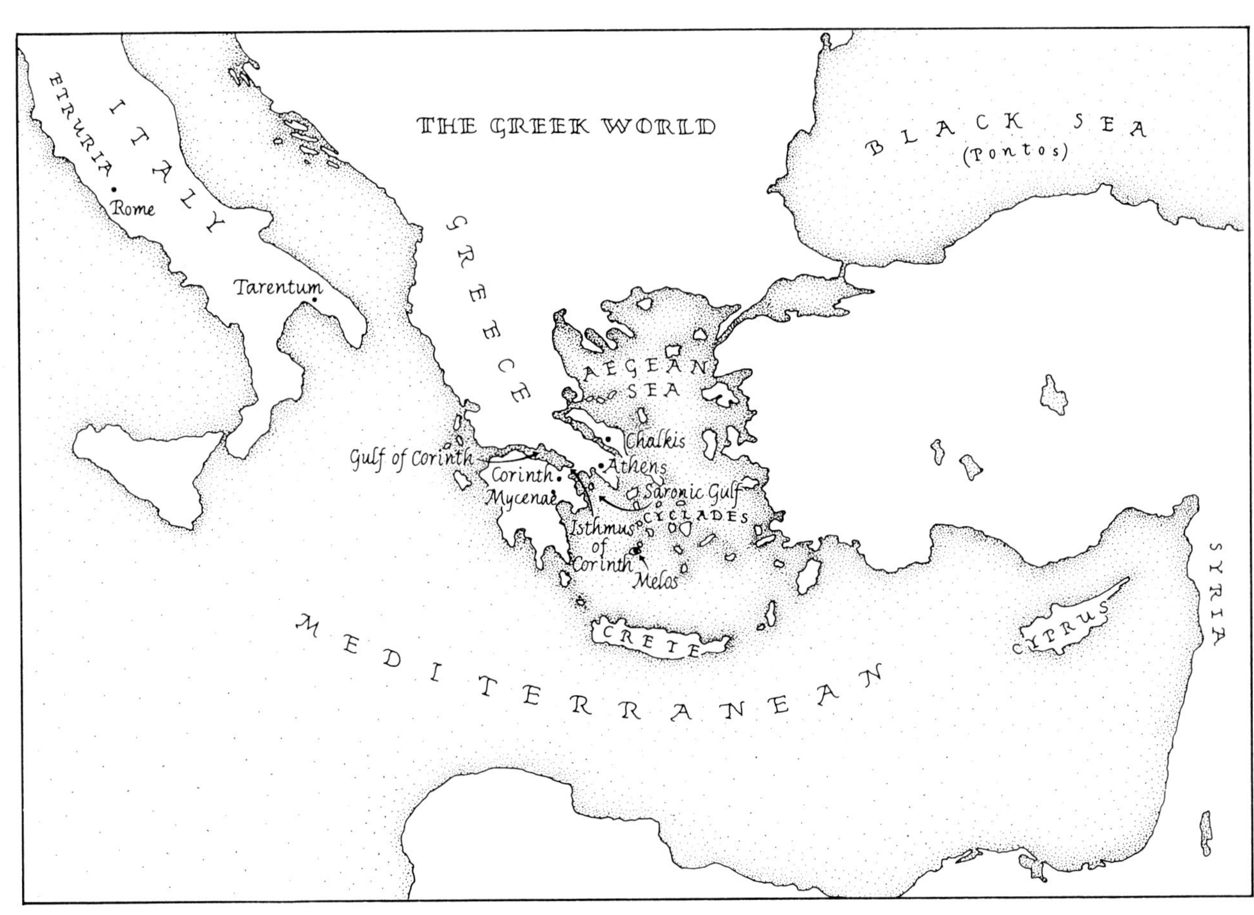
THE GREEK WORLD
ETRURIA
ITALY
Rome
Tarentum
GREECE
BLACK SEA
(Pontos)
AEGEAN
SEA
Chalkis
Athens
Gulf of Corinth
Corinth
Mycenae
Saronic Gulf
CYCLADES
Isthmus
of
Corinth
Melos
CRETE
MEDITERRANEAN
CYPRUS
SYRIA

Introduction

We who frequent museums are people enthralled with the past. In our rationalizing moods we consider the past a guide to the present and the future. But in fact the past is simply fascinating in itself, and the more remote it is, the more intriguing it becomes. To see something ancient at close hand arouses the emotions and stirs the imagination, as though the object actually were able to immerse us in life as it was lived so long ago. When attempting to visualize the role of the object in the lives of those who possessed it, we sense the variety of human experience as one era has melted into another, and that in turn evokes a sense of our own mortality. We take leave of the object feeling different, perhaps better, having been moved by the handiwork of someone whom we can never know personally but who has, if just for a fleeting moment, communicated with us across the ages.

Because the Greeks and Romans played so basic a role in the foundation of Western civilization, Greco-Roman antiquities are especially cherished. Museum patrons in the Pacific Northwest will find a fair number of such antiquities here in the Seattle Art Museum, the majority the generous gifts of Norman and Amelia Davis. The museum's Greco-Roman collection is not extensive, nor does it contain numerous masterpieces. However, these holdings are of good quality and broadly representative. Especially numerous and well preserved are the collection's vases and containers. These convey good information not just about the aesthetic interests of the Greeks and Romans, but also about the techniques of the ancient glass, metallurgical, and ceramic industries. The latter was particularly pervasive, more or less as plastics are in modern times. Not just vases but statuary, household utensils, and even rooftiles and decorative elements for buildings were among the products of ancient craftsmen who worked in clay.

The numerous painted vases in the collection were made with a few simple tools and almost completely of clay. This is true even of the most complex pieces, the vases decorated with black figures on a reddish background, or in red on a black background. All these vessels were made by individuals, most of whom worked in Athens 450 to 550 years before Christ.

In contrast to the anonymous workers who produced all the other vessels in the museum's collection, one delicate little wine cup in the black-figure style (cover illustration) bears the name of the Athenian potter Xenokles. As was the Greek custom, an inscription on the vessel itself proudly announces, "Xenokles made me." Although Xenokles' name occurs on over twenty other surviving pots, we know nothing about him; but we can say something about the conditions under which he worked.

Athenian potters did not work in large factories but in small shops of varying sizes clustered together in the Keramikos (hence ceramics), the name given to the potters' quarter of ancient Athens. The Keramikos is located immediately to the northwest of the Agora or marketplace. Xenokles may have been the shop owner, or perhaps just an employee. This vessel states only that he made its form, but he may also have painted it. We know from the signatures found on black- and red-figure vases that the same craftsman sometimes both threw the vessel and painted it, but it was common for a vessel thrown by one individual to be painted by another. Scholars customarily identify a vessel by the name of its painter if known; if not, the vessel is named after its potter (fig. 19); or, if the potter's name is unknown, by a striking theme on one of an anonymous painter's vases (figs. 18, 20) or by the locality or collection in which a special vase is presently found (figs. 13, 14, 16). In the case of Xenokles' cup, it is thought that not one but two painters decorated it; we cannot know whether one might have been Xenokles himself.

The proverb "potter competes with potter" is quoted by several Greek authors. It indicates that if Xenokles and his fellow potters wanted to stay in business, they had to produce acceptable work on a continuous basis. The competition must have been keen, and we can imagine that Xenokles paid careful attention to the work of his competitors to see how his own measured up. Since work was doubtless displayed outside of shops, and since people have always worked quite openly in the Mediterranean world, there could have been few secrets about vessel shapes or decoration. Everyone doubtless borrowed ideas from everyone else and tried to improve on them. In the end there was only one commodity which could not be borrowed—skill.

Many centuries have passed since Xenokles and his colleagues were at work. Even so, the atmosphere that prevails today among the shops in the Plaka of modern Athens—hot, dusty, crowded, noisy, above all intensely competitive—cannot have been much different from what Xenokles and his colleagues knew.

The products of Xenokles and those who engaged in his trade are remarkably durable and, in contrast to Greek temples and statues, look today pretty much as they did when they were new. No one ever wrote down the methods used to make these pots, but modern researchers have been able to reproduce pieces of this sort very closely. We are satisfied that we can rather accurately describe the process.

Xenokles formed his cup of several parts, each fashioned from a clay that had been soaked in water and a refining agent (perhaps potash) to remove grit and impurities. Fragments of similar cups show how uniform and pure the final fabric is, just as is modern fine china and stoneware. This particular cup consists of the separate elements of bowl, foot, and two handles. The parallel, concentric lines on the surfaces of the bowl and foot show that they were shaped on a potters' wheel. The handles were simply rolled out on a flat surface and bent into shape. The individual pieces were dried briefly and then cemented together with more wet clay.

When the assembled cup was sufficiently dry, Xenokles or some other artist traced and then painted on it—a bull and a deer on the exterior of the bowl, some pal-

Potter fashioning vase on potter's wheel. (From an Attic hydria by the Painter of the Leagros Group in the Glyptothek und Museum antiker Kleinkunst, Munich.)

mettes by the handles, and a hen and rooster on the interior to please and amuse the drinker as the wine was drained. Details on the figures were brought out by incising them with a sharp-pointed instrument. These incisions appear on every black-figure vase in the collection.

The black color of the figures and secondary decorations was produced with a "paint" made of water and the same kind of clay as the fabric of the cup. This solution of clay-paint (called "slip") was obtained through a settling process whereby coarser and heavier clay particles sank and the finer ones, remaining at the top of the clay solution, were drawn off. To the paint was added an agent to keep the fine clay particles from clumping or resettling; vinegar or even urine (a substance widely used by the ancients but completely wasted by us) have been suggested. When the paint had dried, Xenokles burnished the surface of the cup to a glossy finish with some suitable object, such as a pebble.

Some sort of fugitive dye may also have been added to the paint to help distinguish it from the fabric of the cup. Because paint and clay body were so close in color, painters could easily make mistakes. Most red- and black-figure pots feature imperfections of some kind. If you look carefully at the pots in the collection you will find numerous instances in which a figure is not filled in, the paint is distributed unevenly, a line exists where it should not, or vice versa.

In addition to paint that fired black, a sort of purplish red and a white were also used. The former was produced by adding manganese or red ochre to the slip, but the latter was made from a solution of fine white clay. The white was also used as background color for certain types of vessels. Figures 3, 14, and 21 are examples of white-ground pots.

When Xenokles' cup had been painted and allowed to dry, it was placed with other pots in a kiln and fired. Greek potters employed a sophisticated technique of firing, having mastered the manipulation of thermal principles and complex chemical reactions. Firing was a continuous operation that had three stages.

During the first stage (called oxydizing) Xenokles allowed air to circulate freely throughout the kiln via a vent hole on its top. Oxygen in the air combined with the iron naturally present in the clay to

Vase painter at work. (From an Attic hydria by the Leningrad Painter in the Torno Collection, Milan.)

Potter stoking kiln, vent hole at top. (From a Corinthian plaque in the Louvre Museum, Paris.)

produce an orange-red surface on both painted and unpainted parts of the vessel. Clays of different chemical composition might turn buff or light brown (see figs. 4, 7-9, 16).

When the temperature had risen to about 800 degrees Celsius (Xenokles could probably tell just by observing conditions inside the kiln), the second (or reducing) stage of firing commenced. Xenokles now closed the vent and introduced into the fire box some green wood, the effect of which was to reduce greatly the oxygen in the kiln while the temperature rose to as much as 950 degrees Celsius. In this stage the entire surface of the vessel turned black.

At length, as the temperature was declining, Xenokles reopened the vent hole and once again oxygen circulated throughout the kiln in the final (or reoxydizing) stage of the process. At this point the unpainted surface of the vessel once again became orange-red. But the areas that had been coated with black paint, through a complex chemical/physical process achieved during the reducing stage, remained black. Thus was Xenokles' little wine cup created.

The entire process, from wet clay to finished pot, took many days and held numerous pitfalls. Pots could be improperly thrown or carelessly painted; they could become dented or misshapen; their designs could be ruined in drying. While firing, their surfaces could burn if the temperature were too high, or the designs remain matte instead of glossy black if too low. So if all went well, as in this case, Xenokles would have had good reason to be pleased. One might wonder how he would have felt had he known that this cup would survive him by two-and-a-half millenia.

Potter climbing on kiln to close vent hole. (From a Corinthian plaque in the Staatliche Museum, Berlin.)

As Athenian vases were completely handmade and hand decorated, each is unique. Even when the same picture is rendered twice on one vessel (fig. 13), variations always occur. While it was the practice at some times in some places to reproduce unfeelingly the same themes again and again (fig. 9), skilled artisans like Xenokles and his colleagues probably always had ample opportunity to exploit their creative talents and tastes. Their work must have seldom brought on the boredom and rote repetition endured by so many workers on the modern assembly line. While some might regard the limited number of motifs in their repertoire as an impediment, these ancient craftsmen and painters always seemed to find some new way of depicting a well-exploited scene or myth, such as a drinking party (figs. 11, 13, 20). Overall, successful vessel painters must have derived a good deal of professional satisfaction from their work.

Some of them also seem to have gotten rich. There is reason to believe that a cup of the type made by Xenokles sold for several drachmas; one drachma was the daily wage for a skilled laborer in fifth-century Athens. Larger and fancier pots cost more. Pieces such as this cup were, after all, decorative as well as functional, the equivalent in those days of our fine china. When not in use they could be prominently displayed. That is why Xenokles' cup has large handles; they made it possible to suspend the piece from a wall peg.

The appeal of Athenian black- and red-figure vases went far beyond the boundaries of Athens. Eventually they were marketed throughout all of Greece; by the mid-sixth century their popularity caused the demise of the ceramic industries in other states like Corinth, whose wares (figs. 7-9) had previously enjoyed a high regard and a very widespread distribution. Many Athenian pots were valued by non-Greeks, in particular by the Etruscans, the ancient rivals of Rome. Among the Etruscans they were not only used by the living but were also employed as grave furnishings for the dead. That is why so many fine specimens of Athenian pottery are found in Italy. In fact Xenokles' cup is from an Etruscan grave, and this is probably the case with many other black- and red-figure pieces in the collection.

The widespread popularity of Athenian wares encouraged some local entrepreneurs to try to capitalize on their appeal by producing and marketing imitations. This was done both in Greece and in Italy, sometimes with good results (fig. 15), sometimes not (fig. 16). We observe the same sort of thing today in the widespread imitation, and even counterfeiting, of name brands and designer products. In this regard people have been playing a familiar game for centuries.

Athenian pottery merits thorough discussion here because it occupies such an important place in the ancient ceramic industry, and also forms the backbone of the museum's collection. But many other vessels in the collection possess interesting features. Some date to the Bronze Age, others to the period of the Roman Empire. Some are of clay, some of metal, one is stone, one, a Roman funerary urn, is glass. Each exemplifies a particular technology, each played some essential role in everyday human life, and some pieces even illustrate an aspect of life in their time. These vessels have borne their heritage to us across many centuries, and bring with them a rich legacy of insight and beauty.

Bronze Age (3000-1100 B.C.)

1.* Cycladic marble vase
c. 2500 B.C.
H: 3 ¼″
63.71

Cycladic female figurine, marble, c. 2500 B.C.
SAM 64.126

Before they were ever populated by Greeks, the Cycladic Islands were occupied by immigrants from the East who achieved a high degree of culture as early as 3000 B.C. A curiously abstract—almost modern—statuette (SAM 64.126) is an example of their work in marble; so is this delicate little vase. To make it, the craftsman blocked out the exterior using hard stones for shaping tools, and ground the surface smooth with sand or emery; then the interior was hollowed out with a drill bow and smoothed with the same abrasives.

Owing to its tiny size, this vase was probably never intended to be more than a grave embellishment, a miniature of larger clay vessels which the deceased had used in life, and was perhaps thought to need in death. In a full-size pot, the lug handles allowed the pot to be suspended (fig. 4).

Much of what we know of these early Cycladic people is based on objects extracted from their graves. Eventually they and their artistic capabilities were absorbed into the racial stock that became the Greeks of the classical period.

*All pieces illustrated in this catalogue are from the Norman and Amelia Davis Classical Collection.

2. Cycladic kernos
(said to come from Melos)
2200-1900 B.C.
Angular designs in red and brown matte paint on a white slip
H: 7 ½″
63.118

This curious object resembling a candelabrum was hand-fashioned of clay and decorated with a few simple angular patterns. A number of these Cycladic productions have survived, but the use to which they were put has not been proved to everyone's satisfaction. The most plausible suggestion is that they were meant to hold offerings of various fruits and grains for religious ceremonies. This suggestion is attractive because Greek sources of a later time describe similar devices that were employed in this way. To these they give the name "kernos," so the term is applied here as well.

3. Cypriot cup
1600-1450 B.C.
White-slip ware; lozenges and parallel lines in matte brown and brownish orange on a white slip
H: 4″
55.23

Cyprus, too, had received an infusion of Eastern people in the Early Bronze Age, and a distinct native culture was subsequently established. One of its productions is this cup with a wishbone handle, a type which survives in fair numbers.

Like the Cycladic kernos (fig. 2), it is shaped by hand, but its uneven surface, asymmetrical shape, and casual decor make it less impressive than the complex kernos.

The maker of the cup fashioned it of grey clay, which he covered with the thick white paint, or slip, from which the name of this ware is derived. On this, designs were painted in brown and brownish orange (probably a diluted version of the brown); then the piece was fired.

4. Mycenaean amphora
1300-1200 B.C.
Stylized shells and stones; reddish brown paint on a buff background
H: 8 ½″
63.70

In contrast to the kernos and cup (figs. 2 and 3), but like most of the pots in the collection, this amphora, manufactured towards the end of the Bronze Age, was thrown on a wheel. The numerous parallel lines visible on its surface clearly demonstrate this.

The three shoulder lugs allowed the pot to be suspended. (The miniature vase, fig. 1, also has this feature.) The clay in these vessels is to a degree porous, allowing some evaporation to occur when filled with liquid; this in turn cools the contents—a boon in the hot Grecian summer.

This type of amphora was produced all over the Greek world in the later Bronze Age. The homogeneous nature of the pottery shows that a common culture existed at this time. The term "Mycenaean" refers to Mycenae in the northeast Peloponnesos, the most impressive Bronze Age site and home of the Homeric hero Agamemnon.

Early Archaic Period
Geometric Phase, 1050-700 B.C.

5. Athenian pyxis
750-700 B.C.
Geometric patterns and waterfowl; brownish black figures against a light orange background
H: 6 ¼″
63.69

As the earliest Athenian production in the collection, this container was the predecessor of the wares of Xenokles and his fellow potters. Authors of a later age tell us that women used the pyxis as a container for cosmetics and toilet articles. This piece was doubtless the cherished property of a well-to-do woman of Athens and went with her to the grave.

The designs used by the Greeks to decorate pots and other objects from the eleventh up to the seventh centuries B.C. are geometric patterns; hence this period is commonly called 'Geometric.' When animals or men are represented, they are merely geometric silhouettes (as in the procession of waterfowl that forms the upper band of decoration) lacking depth and detail. During this period, man seemed to see himself as an entity of very limited capabilities, rather like the Homeric heroes whose actions are so often dictated not by their desires, but by those of the gods. In fact, the Homeric poems were assuming their final forms at the time this pyxis was made.

Cypro-Archaic, 750-475 B.C.

6. Cypriot barrel flask
700-600 B.C.
Bichrome ware; geometric patterns, bird; black and red matte paint on cream slip
H: 12 ⅜″
54.42

Although this flask was probably not made within the time-frame that scholars assign to Geometric, its flavor is essentially of that style. The vessel demonstrates that enthusiasm for geometric decor persisted longer in some places, and also that Geometric period wares, intended as they were for local consumption, varied a great deal. This Cypriot barrel flask, for example, is decorated with geometric patterns and figures like the Athenian pyxis (fig. 5) but is quite different in the type and color of its designs.

The main figure is apparently a sea bird, as it seems to have a fish in its beak.

The shape of the flask is attractive but, with its rounded bottom, somewhat impractical. Doubtless some sort of collar or stand was needed to keep it upright.

Orientalizing Phase, 700-500 B.C.

7. Corinthian kylix
c. 600 B.C.
Sirens, goat, panthers; brownish black and purple on buff background
H: 3 ½ ″
63.68

In the seventh century many Greek states established extensive foreign commercial contacts. As a result, outside influences, particularly from the East, began to emerge in decoration. Eastern motifs such as palmettes, lotuses, griffins, and the rosettes and panthers on the present piece began to appear on Greek pottery. For this reason we refer to the art works produced in this period as 'Orientalizing.'

During this time the city of Corinth became an important commercial center. Situated on the Isthmus, she was the focus of land traffic running north and south. Through harbors on both the Gulf of Corinth and the Saronic Gulf, Corinth carried on extensive trade by sea to the east and west, particularly with the Italian peoples. This cup was probably extracted from an Etruscan tomb and represents one item in the flood of Corinthian pottery that found its way to Italian soil.

Like Xenokles' cup, the decorations on this piece are painted in black and purple with incised details. The idea of incising may have come from metalwork (compare the ornamentation of the Etruscan mirror, SAM 48.36). In any case, it is clear that the basic techniques employed by Xenokles were established well before his time.

Etruscan mirror, bronze, 4th-3rd century B.C.
SAM 48.36

Through her extensive commercial dealings Corinth became very wealthy. In a sense she was the Paris of the Greco-Roman world, famous for luxury items like perfumes and featuring the only temple prostitutes on the Greek mainland. Her reputation as a center of pleasure persisted for centuries: Plato thought Corinthian women dangerously attractive; the proverb "Not everyone should go to Corinth" meant that a good time in Corinth cost plenty.

Understandably, Corinth's commercial interests influenced the type of pottery she manufactured. Since perfumes and cosmetics were important in Greek culture, many small delicate containers were in demand. Our collection contains a fair sample of them, including this little pyxis. It is much more dainty than the earlier Athenian pyxis (fig. 5). The paint has not always fired a uniform black but is reddish in places.

8. Corinthian pyxis
c. 600 B.C.
Birds and panthers; black against a buff background
H: 2 ½″
67.122

9. Corinthian aryballos
575-550 B.C.
Warriors carrying clubs and shields; brownish black and purple against a buff background
H: 1¼″
67.121

The Corinthians, apparently realizing that they had a good thing going, proceeded to manufacture pots as quickly as they could. As a result, they must have created something like the first assembly line, as every effort was made to produce a fixed repertoire of figures and secondary designs in the simplest way. The parade of club-wielding warriors on this piece is a good example. Intended perhaps to represent the bodyguard of a Corinthian tyrant, the figures are rendered with a few painted circles and straight lines and a limited amount of incision. They clearly required little skill to execute, much less talent, and are typical of a formulaic treatment of design elements.

In any case, the benefit to the Corinthians of mass production was offset by the dullness and monotony of what they produced. Here the draughtsmanship also seems skewed: either the warriors are looking over their shoulders with their shields on their right instead of left arms, or their feet are painted backwards! These deficiencies gave the more exacting Athenian potters their chance; with their superior wares they soon captured the international market once dominated by the Corinthians. (The skyphos, fig. 10, embodies the difference in Athenian and Corinthian ware.)

The aryballos was used especially by athletes to hold olive oil for bathing. Often a thong was looped through its handle so that it could be suspended from the wrist.

Later Archaic to Classical, 550-323 B.C.

The Athenians inherited and used the Corinthian technique of painting and incising figures in black and purple against a lighter background. Their own work, however, quickly demonstrated much greater vigor and imagination. They soon became preoccupied with representing scenes from mythology and everyday life. Perhaps people eventually came to prefer Athenian rather than Corinthian pots not only because their sharp colors (though the black has not always fired well here), deft draughtsmanship, and numerous shapes had greater appeal, but also because their decoration gave one so much more to talk about. The owner of this piece, for example, set before his guests a vessel featuring not a wooden procession of bodyguards or animals, but one with familiar scenes from the *Iliad*, which were bound to arouse comment.

The skyphos is a large-capacity vessel and is frequently portrayed in party scenes. As it is larger than, say, Xenokles' delicate cup, heartier drinkers like Herakles (Hercules) and Dionysos, god of wine, are often pictured holding them.

10. Athenian black-figure skyphos
540-530 B.C.
Thetis entreats Zeus on behalf of Achilles, Achilles dons the armour of Hephaistos
Painter of the Nicosia Olpe
H: 5⅝″
65.155

11. Athenian black-figure amphora
525-500 B.C.
Dancing women, partying men
Leagros Group
H: 17⅛″
63.119

The amphora is one of the most common vessel types. Large undecorated ones were used to store, age, and transport various provisions, such as pickled products, oil, and wine. Smaller decorated models like this one served as temporary containers for the same items.

It is easy to imagine that this large and ornately decorated amphora was intended to hold wine, as the dancing ladies and gentlemen fit the drinking theme well. The male revelers in particular appear to be feeling no pain, and one carries a standard drinking vessel, the rhyton (see fig. 22). If this pot were so employed, it probably originally had a lid (see fig. 15). Many similar pieces are preserved with their lids intact.

Black-figure vessels belonging to the Leagros Group were produced just as red-figure ware (fig. 18) was becoming fashionable, and perhaps in the same workshop. Influenced by red-figure work, their pictures are remarkably supple and lifelike. The name of this group derives from the kalos name (see fig. 19), Leagros, borne by a number of its pots.

Detail of apotropaic eye

12. Athenian black-figure kyathos
525-500 B.C.
The return of Hephaistos to Olympos
H: 6⅛″
64.127

It is readily apparent that many of the potters' fine productions were designed for drinking wine. This ladle must have been so intended, to judge by its decorative figures—a dancing satyr and Dionysos, god of wine. Dionysos holds a rhyton, yet another drinking vessel (see fig. 22).

The theme portrayed here is very likely the return of Hephaistos. The kernel of the myth is that Hephaistos, the crippled artisan-god, was thrown out of Olympos by Zeus for siding with Hera in a family quarrel (a frequent occurrence). Hephaistos then lived nine years on the Isle of Lemnos, but eventually Dionysos succeeded in retrieving him, with the aid of wine, of course. Usually Hephaistos was depicted accompanied by a throng of drunken and aroused satyrs and animals led by Dionysos. But on a small vessel, as here, the painter shortened the story, portraying only one satyr, one appropriately erect donkey (perhaps with Hephaistos aboard) and naturally, one tipsy Dionysos.

The painter also provided an "eye." Such painted eyes appear frequently on pots. They have to do with the concept of the "evil eye" which survives today in Mediterranean lands. The Greeks thought the eye was originally that of the Gorgon, whose gaze turned men to stone. They also imagined that the eye could be used to ward off bad luck; hence, it is often called an apotropaic device, after the Greek word for "turn away." The purpose of the eye on wine vessels is probably to keep away thundering hangovers.

13. Athenian black-figure stamnos
525-500 B.C.
Party scenes, chariot races
Attributed to the Michigan Painter
H: 10 ½″
66.47

The stamnos is basically an amphora and was used for the same purposes (see fig. 11). It was a shape especially popular in Italy and Sicily, where this example probably was found. This stamnos illustrates the practice of sometimes painting the same theme on both sides of a vessel, but as Greek painters worked freehand, the pictures usually vary somewhat, as here.

The symposium (drinking party) theme is easily identified because Greeks of means were not in the habit of drinking with their wives; women depicted in drinking scenes on Greek vessels were courtesans.

Sporting scenes are popular on stamnoi decorated by the Michigan Painter. Perhaps they were meant to hold olive oil and were given as prizes for athletic achievement. This was the case with a special type of amphora made in Athens and awarded to winners in the Panathenaic Games. As it happens, the Michigan Painter also decorated panathenaic amphoras.

14. Athenian black-figure oinochoe
500-480 B.C.
Non-Greek warriors on horse and foot
Name piece of the Seattle Group
H: 9″
63.66

When a painter's name is unknown, his work is sometimes identified by the modern location of one of his vessels. The same procedure is often followed when several pots have common characteristics and should be classified together, even though they may be the work of more than one painter (compare to the Leagros Group, fig. 11). One can only wonder how the painters of a series of surviving pots would have reacted had they realized that someday their work would be dubbed the "Seattle Group."

The distinguishing features of vessels in the Seattle Group are well illustrated by their name piece, this oinochoe (or wine pitcher). All are in the black-figure style, but are painted against a white background, and they are all wine pitchers of a distinct character.

The fact that the figures decorating the vessel wear pants immediately distinguishes them from the Greeks, who recoiled at what seemed to them barbaric dress. In the early fifth century the Athenians had dealings with the Scythians, nomads from the steppes, who wore such apparel. So did the Amazons, those very liberated women of mythology, who were sometimes used as symbols for foreign invaders, such as the Persians. Both are good candidates for the identification of the barbarian warriors depicted here.

15. Lid of Chalcidian krater
c. 530 B.C.
Lotuses and sirens
D: 12 ⅜″
65.117

The widespread appeal of Athenian pottery encouraged imitation, some of it very good. Most of us would be hard pressed to distinguish this piece from the Athenian black-figure pots in the collection. One clue is the chain of plump lotus flowers and buds which Chalcidian painters favored. This lid was originally used to cover a krater, a large open vessel in which wine was mixed with water, flavorings, and spices. Greeks rarely drank their wine neat; many southern Europeans today prefer to dilute it with water.

We call this ware "Chalcidian" because the alphabet and dialect in inscriptions on some pieces seem to indicate as its source the city of Chalkis on the island of Euboea. However, no example has ever been found east of the Adriatic, whereas a great deal has been recovered in Italy. It would seem then that some Greeks from Chalkis may have set up shop in Italy and manufactured this ware to take advantage of the extensive market the Athenians enjoyed there, especially among the Etruscans.

16. Pontic oinochoe
c. 530 B.C.
Riding and hunting scenes; reddish brown and red on buff
Attributed to the Paris Painter
H: 11 ¾″
59.82

Less successful in imitating Athenian black-figure ware is this Etruscan oinochoe (compare fig. 14), a sample of the so-called Pontic ware. Pontic ware is so named because those who first studied it thought that it was manufactured by Greeks living on the Black Sea (Pontos in Greek). In fact this type of pottery is not found outside of Etruscan territory and seems, like Chalcidian ware, to have been produced for mostly local consumption, though in this case by non-Greeks. Connoisseurs are, understandably, not so impressed with the draughtsmanship and muddy colors of Pontic ware; on the other hand, the scenes painted here possess an attractive vigor. One panel on this vessel is especially interesting because it depicts the nets and throwing sticks used in hunting hare.

An apotropaic eye appears here on the spout (see also fig. 12).

17. Etruscan bronze oinochoe
5th century B.C.
H: 10 ¾″
62.156

Etruscan drinking vessel, Bucchero ware, pottery, 600-575 B.C. *SAM 63.90*

What might the Etruscans have offered in exchange for the Athenian pottery that they imported? There was a type of native ceramic ware called Bucchero, of which the collection possesses a fine example (SAM 63.90). But, while Bucchero was exported to the East, it seems not to have been sent out in great quantity. When Greek wares became popular in Italy, Bucchero production eventually ceased. In short, pottery is not the answer.

Metals and metalwork may have provided the export exchange. The Etruscans earned high marks among the ancients in many aspects of metalwork, especially when it came to household goods. This bronze oinochoe is a fine example, one of many such specimens that have survived.

To make this oinochoe an Etruscan craftsman soldered together three separate pieces: body, base, and handle. There is a seam close to the base and evidence of soldering where the handle joins the rim. Base and handle are heavy and were therefore cast in molds; the body, which is of thinner metal, was probably created from a sheet of bronze beaten into the desired shape.

18. Athenian red-figure hydria
c. 450 B.C.
Hermes, Apollo, and Artemis with unidentified attendants
Nausicaa Painter
H: 14 ⅝″
68.6

Beginning in the later sixth century the Athenian taste for black figures against a red background was reversed in favor of red figures on a black background. Detail on the figures was no longer rendered by incision, but by brush-applied lines and washes of thick and thinned-out versions of black slip; the secondary colors of purple and white were soon used sparingly.

It is easy to see why the red-figure style came to be preferred. Through it the body and the drapery covering it can be depicted more realistically, as a greater sense of detail and perspective are possible. By the early fifth century, except for a few special vessels, black-figure production ceased in Athens.

The hydria is basically an amphora with three handles. Its primary use, as its name suggests, is for carrying water. A vertical handle on the back can be used for balancing the vessel on shoulder or head.

Among the figures, Hermes can be identified by his caduceus (we now use it as a symbol of the medical profession), Apollo by his lyre, and his sister Artemis by her bow. After years of mystery, the name of the Nausicaa Painter is now known: on an amphora by his hand in London appears the signature "Polygnotos painted me."

19. Athenian red-figure kylix
c. 500-480 B.C.
Exterior: combat scenes;
interior: discus thrower
After the manner of the Epeleios Painter
H: 5″
82.128

Interior scene: discus thrower

Among the more recent acquisitions of the museum is this splendid cup, which is much larger than the type produced half a century earlier by Xenokles. These large cups were passed around at parties; one drinker was not expected to drain its contents himself!

This piece is particularly interesting in that it has the word "kalos" (handsome, pretty) painted several times along its rim. Athenian pots frequently bear similar inscriptions, often along with a personal name. (A personal name may also have been painted here; but, if so, it has not yet been deciphered.) The purpose of these inscriptions was obviously to praise the beauty of aristocratic youth in the highly bisexual atmosphere of upper-class Athens. One of the most frequently praised young men was Leagros, and his name has been given to an entire group of pots, one of them an amphora in the museum's collection (fig. 11).

It is natural that athletics and warfare are here depicted together. For the Greeks athletic conditioning was a necessary prerequisite for the heavy work of wielding spears and swords. Elsewhere in the collection are objects used by soldier-athletes, including a splendid helmet (SAM 84.169) and a bronze body scraper (SAM 64.157). The latter was used to remove olive oil, with which athletes anointed themselves, and the dust and sweat mixed with it after a vigorous workout.

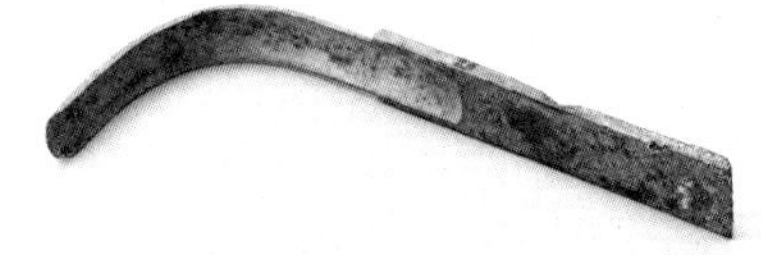

Greek body scraper, bronze, 5th or 4th century B.C.
SAM 64.157

This red-figure cup is an especially fine piece—its line and detail express impressive vigor. A group of drinkers is depicted carrying a vessel called a skyphos, of which there are several in the collection (see fig. 10). Small tassels appear at the corners of the revelers' drapelike garments. These tassels served both as decorations and as weights to help the drapery hang properly. Also depicted is a staff of the sort Athenian dandies carried around, leaned on, and even used to hitch up their loose-fitting clothing.

On the interior is depicted a party game called "kottabos." Its object was to fling the dregs of the wine which collected in the bottom of cups into a container, or even at some object. A wish could be made in advance; the idea was that if the target were hit, the wish would come true. The large handles of the cups made the game possible.

Also painted in various places are letters which make no sense. Inscriptions other than signatures and kalos names often occur on pots. Some identify the subject(s), others are mottoes or slogans; an especially jaunty one is "Hi, drink up!" But often, as here, letters are randomly strung along the surface. It could be that the painter was simply illiterate, and unwilling to play second fiddle to those of his competitors who were not, he learned to reproduce letters but not words.

Interior scene: kottabos game

20. Athenian red-figure kylix
500-480 B.C.
Exterior and interior: party scenes; purplish red fillets and garlands
Painter of the Paris Gigantomachia
H: 5″
59.30

21. Athenian white-ground lekythos

420-400 B.C.
Woman holding a wreath before a flaming altar; various shades of brown against a white background
H: 8″
70.101

A lekythos is a small container for oil or perfume. Many are decorated with figures painted against a white background (black figures thus executed are seen in fig. 14). In these cases both white background and black to brown to orange paint were applied before firing in the usual three-part process. Sometimes blues, reds, and yellows were also used; such colors were applied after firing and are less permanent. If these colors were ever painted on the present piece, they are gone now.

In many instances these vessels were left as offerings to the dead, and a number of lekythoi actually depict tombs covered with them. Eventually, some tomb markers came to assume the lekythos shape. One such mortuary lekythos in stone is part of the collection, having once graced the resting place of an Athenian girl, Aristonike, daughter of Aristeides (SAM 55.204).

Greek grave marker in shape of a lekythos, marble, c. 350-300 B.C. *SAM 55.204*

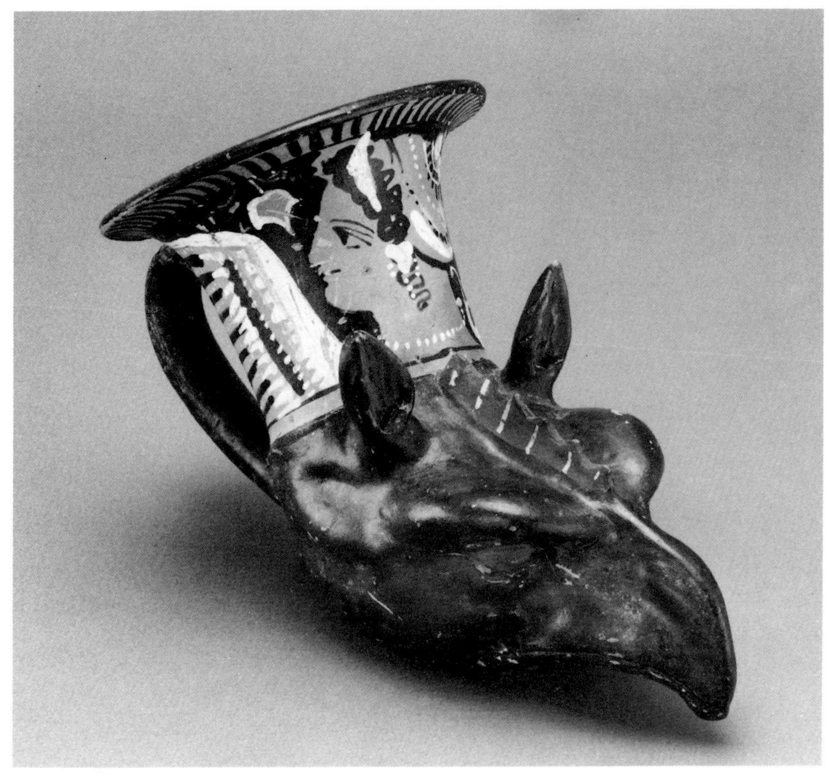

22. Tarentine red-figure rhyton
350-330 B.C.
Eros or Nike, mounted on the head of a griffin
L: 7 ½″
67.120

The rhyton is a drinking vessel curved like a horn. It often appears in depictions of drinking scenes (see figs. 11 and 12). Frequently it is shaped like an animal's head. Astydamas, a poet of the fourth century B.C., specifically refers to one in the form of a griffin.

The upper portion of this piece was manufactured in the usual manner for red-figure pots. The griffin base was either hand shaped, or shaped in a terra cotta mold which itself had been based on a clay model; then it was painted, attached to the upper section, and the resulting ensemble fired.

This rhyton was made in southern Italy where the local Greeks imitated Athenian red-figure ware, just as previously there had been imitations of black-figure ware (see figs. 15 and 16 for Chalcidian and Etruscan examples). South Italian red-figure ware is usually quite distinct from the Athenian: the muddy or greenish nature of the "black" paint seldom measures up to Athenian standards, a lot of white is used, and the draughtsmanship is not as good.

A Nike, which to us is a missile or a running shoe, was to the Greeks a winged female figure representing victory; Eros (Cupid) was, of course, the son of Aphrodite (Venus), the goddess of love. The painters of these rhytons regularly outfitted both their Cupids and Nikes with chignons and earrings, making precise identification impossible when, as here, only the figure's head is shown.

The earrings worn by the figure remind us that the Greeks were excellent jewellers; in fact, the collection possesses a number of earrings, including a fine set from the fourth century (SAM 60.26).

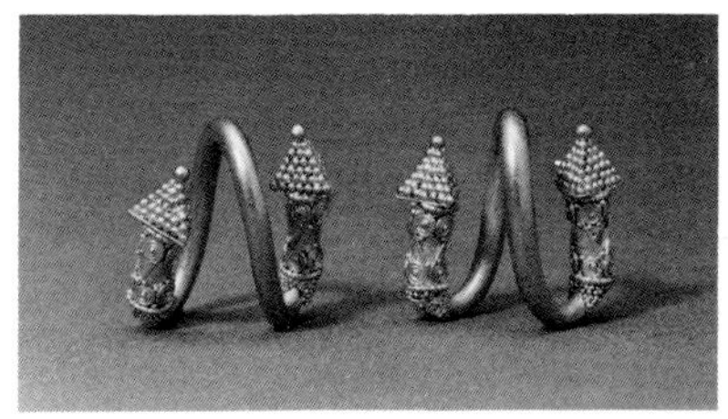

Greek earrings, gold, 325-300 B.C. *SAM 60.26*

Roman Empire

23. Roman glass funerary urn
(said to come from Syria)
1st to 2nd century A.D.
H: 12 ¾″
56.64

The purpose of this urn was to hold the cremated remains of the dead.

The body of the vessel was blown free (i.e., not in a mold) as its assymmetry shows. To make it, the craftsman collected some molten glass (gather) on the end of an iron tube; by blowing into the tube he created the bubble which we see now. The lid and handles were fashioned with a solid iron rod (pontil) on the end of which the gather was collected and shaped. The lid is complex and must have been reheated and reshaped a number of times. The handles were a simpler matter. For each, the gather was attached to the shoulder of the vessel, drawn out in a loop, and then attached at a second point. In both cases the gather did not completely detach itself from the pontil at the end of the manoeuver; thus, when the craftsman pressed the remaining gather onto the handles, he created what now look like seams.

The art of blowing glass was invented in the first century B.C., perhaps in Syria where this piece is said to have been found. After that time glass, which had been a luxury item, could be cheaply mass produced. Many objects which previously had been made of clay could now be made of glass, and so the ceramic industry was curtailed. This urn is therefore not only one of the latest items in the collection from a chronological point of view, but it attests the decline of one technology in favor of another.